A Book of Vestry Pray

A BOOK OF VESTRY PRAYERS

COMPILED BY

C. N. R. WALLWORK

EPWORTH PRESS

7162 0277 8

First published 1976
by Epworth Press
Room 195, 1 Central Buildings
Westminster, London SW1
Fifth impression 1995

Printed and bound in Great Britain by
Mackays of Chatham PLC, Chatham, Kent

I dedicate this little book to three friends

STELLA BUCKLEY

D. CONLEY EADES

and

ARTHUR S. GREGORY

whose protestant devotion
to the catholic faith
set me down
in the
universe
of the church's written prayers

Contents

Foreword

THE compiler of this collection of prayers has an eye for sources and an ear for prose: he has dug treasures from ancient mines; he has sifted through much modern dross and has found a few jewels. Not only that; he has also tried his hand at writing: and we are grateful to him both for some prayers in the form and language of the traditional collects, and for some with a newer look. By their conciseness and their doctrinal exactness, these last may help towards the creation of a standard in style and content which contemporary compositions as yet largely lack. Stewards and preachers who make this collection their own will find their praying much enriched: such has been my experience in following the growth of this book.

GEOFFREY WAINWRIGHT

Preface

THE origin of this book was a request from the Revd John Stacey and the Revd Dr Geoffrey Wainwright, but it is the result of a sustained interest in the written prayers of the Church and a firm conviction that the Free Church tradition is impoverished wherever it limits itself to the valued and important ministry of extempore prayer.

My pleasure in compiling this collection of prayers has been increased by the help and encouragement which I have received from my wife, Margaret, from friends and colleagues and from the stewards of Norley Central Methodist Church. I am particularly grateful for the thorough and willing help of Canon Colquhoun who so courteously and promptly responded to my requests for assistance and for the critical and welcome advice of Mr W. Jardine Grisbrooke.

The book owes much to the constant and discerning comments and suggestions which Dr Wainwright has given at every stage of the work, not only with regard to the new prayers within these pages but also with regard to the contents of the book itself.

C.N.R.W.

Introduction

THE busy minutes which precede an act of worship are precious. They can either contribute to the service or detract from it. To ensure that these prayers bring the greatest possible blessing, the following points should be noted.

Two prayers are provided for each Sunday or special day. The first prayer is written in a classical form and the second in a contemporary form. Where there are two Sunday services, it may be thought suitable to use both prayers during the course of the day.

The appropriate prayer should be chosen well in advance and read through before it is used. This will ensure that its meaning is clear both to the one who reads it and to those who will listen. This method also enables the prayer to come from the heart.

This collection of prayers is in two parts. The first part consists of prayers for the ordinary course of the Christian calendar. The second part of this collection consists of prayers for special services in the life of the local church.

On the major Holy Days,* only the appropriate prayers are said, even if there is a baptism or confirmation.

Church diaries, official minutes and yearbooks, the religious press and preaching plans usually indicate the appropriate titles for each Sunday. A regular check will avoid any confusion.

* Christmas Day, Good Friday, Easter Day, Ascension Day, Whitsunday, Trinity Sunday and All Saints' Day.

Ideally there are five stages to each prayer.

1 The bidding "Let us pray"
2 A short silence
3 The Prayer
4 The Amen
5 Another short silence

Lent, 1976 C. N. R. WALLWORK

Part One

PRAYERS FOR THE CHURCH'S YEAR

Ninth Sunday before Christmas

FIFTH BEFORE ADVENT

Almighty Father, whose mercy is as thy majesty:
Fill us with reverence, as we come before thee,
for thine exceeding glory: and with love, for
thine exceeding love; through Jesus Christ our
Lord. *Amen*

Eric Milner-White and G. W. Briggs

O God, who in the work of creation
commanded the light to shine out of darkness:
we pray that the light of the glorious gospel of Christ
may shine into the hearts of men everywhere,
dispelling the darkness of their ignorance and unbelief
and revealing to them the knowledge of your glory
in the face of Jesus Christ our Lord. *Amen*

Based on 2 Corinthians 4:4–6

Eighth Sunday before Christmas

FOURTH BEFORE ADVENT

Almighty and everlasting God, the source and
perfection of all virtues: Grant us this day
so to honour thy name and so to preach thy
truth that we may afford to thy faithful people
the instruction which is of thy grace; through
Jesus Christ our Lord. *Amen*

After a prayer from the Leonine Sacramentary

God of power and mercy,
only with your help
can we offer you fitting service and praise.
May we live the faith we profess
and trust your promise of eternal life.
Grant this through our Lord Jesus Christ, your Son,
who lives and reigns with you and the Holy Spirit,
one God, for ever and ever. *Amen*

The Sunday Missal

Seventh Sunday before Christmas

THIRD BEFORE ADVENT

O Great King of heaven and earth: As we draw near to thy throne of grace in the name of Jesus Christ, cast out all evil from within us; grant us holiness, wisdom and spiritual understanding; that increasing in knowledge of thy love, we may be fruitful in every good work; through the same Christ our Lord. *Amen*

After Bishop Jeremy Taylor, 1667

O God, most holy, most loving, infinite in wisdom and power: teach us to reverence you in all the works of your hands, and to hallow your name both in our lives and in our worship; through Jesus Christ our Lord. *Amen*

New Every Morning

Sixth Sunday before Christmas

SECOND BEFORE ADVENT

O God, who hast given us ears to hear thy word,
and tongues to praise thee: Cleanse our hearts,
that we may be obedient to the word which we hear;
and our lips, that we may worship thee in truth;
for Jesus Christ's sake. *Amen*

Eric Milner-White and G. W. Briggs

Almighty God our heavenly Father, at your call we come reverently to worship you. May your Holy Spirit be with us, teaching us to recognize your goodness and truth, and helping us to praise you, not only with words, but with lives which are obedient to you; through your Son, Jesus Christ. *Amen*

Together in Church

Fifth Sunday before Christmas

THE SUNDAY BEFORE ADVENT

Eternal Light, shine into our hearts,
Eternal Goodness, deliver us from evil,
Eternal Power, be our support,
Eternal Wisdom, scatter the darkness of our ignorance,
Eternal Pity, have mercy upon us;
that with all our heart and mind and soul and strength
we may seek thy face
and be brought by thine infinite mercy
to thy holy presence;
through Jesus Christ our Lord. *Amen*

Alcuin A D *735–804*

Lord you spoke by the prophets, and you have spoken
to us in your Son: guide our minds by your Spirit,
that we may understand your word. May it prove in us
and in the world a word of life and power, through
the same Jesus Christ. *Amen*

New Every Morning

Fourth Sunday before Christmas

ADVENT I

Almighty God our heavenly Father, send, we beseech thee, thy Holy Spirit into our hearts, that we may be directed and controlled according to thy will, led into all truth, defended from all sin, and enriched in all grace; through Jesus Christ our Lord. *Amen*

The Book of Worship

O God, our Judge and Saviour, set before us the vision of your purity, and let us see our sins in the light of your holiness. Pierce our self-contentment with the shafts of your burning love, and let that love consume in us all that hinders us from perfect service of your cause; for as your holiness is our judgement, so are your wounds our salvation. *Amen*

New Every Morning

Third Sunday before Christmas

ADVENT 2

Almighty and most merciful God, who hast given the Bible to be the revelation of thy great love to man, and of thy power and will to save him; grant that our study of it may not be in vain by the callousness or the carelessness of our hearts, but that by it we may be confirmed in penitence, lifted to hope, made strong for service, and, above all, be filled with the true knowledge of thee and of thy Son Jesus Christ. *Amen*

George Adam Smith

Grant, O Lord, that in the written Word, and through the spoken Word, we may behold the living Word, our Saviour Jesus Christ. *Amen*

Simon H. Baynes

Second Sunday before Christmas

ADVENT 3

Almighty God, who dost send thy messengers to prepare thy way before thee: Endue with the power of the Holy Spirit all who go forth to preach and speak in thy name. Touch their hearts; enlighten their minds; cleanse and instruct their lips; give them a clear vision of thy will and purpose for the whole world; and through their voice do thou call back thy Church to simpler discipleship, readier obedience, and more loving service; through thy Son Jesus Christ our Lord. *Amen*

Peter Green

By your power, Sovereign Lord,
John the Baptist was born into the world
as forerunner of the promised Messiah:
Help us to heed his message
of repentance and amendment of life,
and to follow his example
of boldness and self-denial;
through Jesus Christ our Lord. *Amen*

Collects with the New Lectionary

The Sunday before Christmas

ADVENT 4

Almighty and everlasting God, the Light of the faithful and the Ruler of souls, who hast hallowed us by the incarnation of thy Word, and the child-bearing of the Blessed Virgin Mary; we beseech thee, let the power of thy Holy Spirit come also upon us, and the mercy of the Highest overshadow us. *Amen*

Mozarabic Missal

Almighty God, Mary gave birth to a Son who offers salvation to the whole world. May we, like Mary, both treasure him in our hearts and bring him to all men, through the same Christ our Lord. *Amen*

A Christian's Prayer Book

Christmas Eve

O God, who hast hallowed this sacred night
with the joyful tidings of the Word made flesh:
Grant us so to venerate the mystery of Christ's
glory upon the earth, that we may at the last
behold him face to face, in the fulness of his
eternal glory in heaven; through the same Jesus
Christ our Lord. *Amen*

C. N. R. Wallwork

Lord Jesus Christ,
Child of Bethlehem and Son of God:
help us this night
to join our songs of glory
to those of the heavenly host,
that the joy of the church on earth
may be heard in the praise of heaven. *Amen*

C. N. R. Wallwork

Christmas Day

Grant unto us, we pray thee, O Lord our God, that we who rejoice to keep the feast of the Nativity of Jesus Christ our Lord, may by walking worthily of him attain to fellowship with him, through the same Jesus Christ our Lord. *Amen*

Leonine Sacramentary

Lord God, you are the Father of mankind. Today you have gathered into one, things earthly and things heavenly through the gift of your beloved Son, our new-born brother. As we travel on this earthly pilgrimage, may your light shine in our hearts, and may we see the glory of Christ, born in our midst. *Amen*

A Christian's Prayer Book

*The Sunday after Christmas**

Almighty and everlasting God, who hast made known the incarnation of thy Word by the testimony of a glorious star, which when the wise men beheld, they adored thy majesty with gifts; grant that the star of thy righteousness may always appear in our hearts, and our treasure consist in giving thanks to thee; through Jesus Christ our Lord. *Amen*

Gelasian Sacramentary

O God our Father, who by the bright shining of a star
led the wise men to the city of David:
guide us by the light of your Spirit,
that we too may come into the presence of Jesus
and offer our gifts and our worship to him,
our Saviour and our Lord. *Amen*

Alan Warren

* If this falls on December 30th, the prayers of the Second Sunday after Christmas are read.

*Second Sunday after Christmas**

O Lord Jesus Christ, Wisdom and Word of God, dwell in our hearts, we beseech thee, by thy most Holy Spirit, that out of the abundance of our hearts our mouths may speak thy praise. *Amen*

Christina Rossetti

Eternal God, all-powerful and merciful,
your word is a torch for our path
and a light for our way.
Open our eyes and enlighten our spirit
that we may understand your revelation
in all its purity and holiness.
May it transform our lives
and make us worthy to bear your image;
through Jesus Christ our Lord. *Amen*

Zwingli

* If this falls on January 6th, the prayers of the Sunday after Christmas are read.

Epiphany

O Lord God, who gavest to wise men of
old a glorious star to lead them to the Christ:
Grant that we to whom thou hast given a
yet more glorious sign, even his holy Cross,
may follow and be led by it the whole way to
our salvation and thy heaven: through the
same Jesus Christ our Lord. *Amen*

Eric Milner-White

Lord Jesus Christ,
King of Glory and Light of the World:
be present in your people's prayers
and shine through their praise,
that the vision of your glory on earth
may lead us to the light of your splendour in heaven. *Amen*

C. N. R. Wallwork

First Sunday after Epiphany

O Lord Jesus Christ, who hast deigned to be made like unto men; the sharer of our sorrows, the companion of our journeys, the light of our ignorance, the remedy of our infirmity: So fill us with thy Spirit, and endue us with thy grace that as thou hast been made like unto us, we may grow more like unto thee; for thy mercy's sake. *Amen*

Eric Milner-White

Father, when Jesus was baptised in the Jordan,
you proclaimed him as your well-beloved Son,
and the Holy Spirit came upon him.
May your Spirit guide and help us
to share in your ministry to men;
through the same Jesus Christ our Lord. *Amen*

A Christian's Prayer Book

Second Sunday after Epiphany

O Lord Jesus Christ, who didst send forth thy first disciples to proclaim thy kingdom, and to teach thy commandments: Give to us thy disciples this day, such an understanding of the word, that we may teach to others what we have been taught of thee; to the glory of thy Name, and the spread of thy Kingdom. *Amen*

Daily Prayer

Lord, all your treasures of wisdom and knowledge are hidden in Christ.
You reveal them to us through words spoken in his name.
May we understand and obey;
for his sake. *Amen*

Contemporary Prayers for Public Worship

Third Sunday after Epiphany

O Lord, we beseech thee mercifully to receive the prayers of thy people which call upon thee; and grant that they may both perceive and know what things they ought to do, and also may have grace and power faithfully to fulfil the same; through Jesus Christ our Lord. *Amen*

Book of Common Prayer

Lord Jesus Christ, divine Word, speak to us now.
Show us the beauty of life; unite us to the eternal purpose; remove our guilt; conquer the fear of death in our hearts.
Speak and let us hear, for your name's sake. *Amen*

Contemporary Prayers for Public Worship

Fourth Sunday after Epiphany

Almighty God, our heavenly Father, whose Son Jesus Christ came to cast fire upon the earth: grant that by the prayers of thy faithful people a fire of burning zeal may be kindled, and pass from heart to heart, till all our hardness is melted in the warmth of thy love; through him who loved us and gave himself for us, Jesus Christ our Lord. *Amen*

G. C. Binyon

Look upon us, O Lord, and let all the darkness of our souls vanish before the beams of your brightness. Fill us with holy love, and open to us the treasures of your wisdom. As we seek your face, show us your glory, that our longing may be satisfied and our peace be perfect; through Jesus Christ our Lord. *Amen*

Adapted from a Prayer of Saint Augustine

Fifth Sunday after Epiphany

Grant us, O Lord, the help of thy Spirit in our hearts, that we may enter into thy holy presence with reverence and gladness, and render a service acceptable unto thee; through Jesus Christ our Lord. *Amen*

The Minister's Prayer Book

Lord Jesus Christ,
Word of God,
Saviour of men
and King of Saints:
accept the worship of your Church
and through its ministry
speak to us,
save us,
and bring us to eternal life;
for your name's sake.
Amen

C. N. R. Wallwork

Sixth Sunday after Epiphany

Almighty God, who hast given a day of rest to thy people, and, through thy Spirit in the Church, hast consecrated the first day of the week to be a perpetual memorial of thy Son's resurrection: Grant that we may so use thy gift that, refreshed and strengthened in soul and body, we may serve thee faithfully all the days of our life; through the same Jesus Christ our Lord. *Amen*

The Book of Worship

Eternal God and Father, in whose presence we find rest and peace: as we come to you now, may we be cleansed and strengthened by your Spirit, and serve you with a quiet mind. *Amen*

New Every Morning

Ninth Sunday before Easter

Help us, O Holy Spirit, Giver of life and love, to be always mindful of the love from whence we came, that we may learn more and more the love to which we go: and in this love abounding, daily abide; through Jesus Christ our Lord. *Amen*

Eric Milner-White

Lord, take our minds and think through them;
take our lips and speak through them;
take our hearts and set them on fire with the desire to do your holy will; in the name of Jesus Christ our Lord. *Amen*

Student Prayer

Eighth Sunday before Easter

Let thy Spirit, O Lord, come into the midst of us, and washing us with the pure water of repentance, prepare us to be always a living sacrifice unto thee; through Jesus Christ our Lord. *Amen*

Mozarabic Missal

Lord,
We thank you for your perpetual presence with your people. May your Holy Spirit bless the ministry of your gracious Word, that we may leave this place enlightened, refreshed and strengthened for the work you have given us to do; for Christ's sake. *Amen*

C. N. R. Wallwork

Seventh Sunday before Easter

Incline thine ear, O Lord, to our prayers, and enlighten the darkness of our minds by the grace of thy visitation: that in thy light we may see light and walk in thy truth without stumbling, and at last attain to the light of life everlasting; through Jesus Christ our Lord. *Amen*

Adapted from Sarum

Lord Jesus, the true bread from heaven who came to give life to the world: satisfy the longings of our hearts and fulfil in us your promise that those who come to you shall hunger and thirst no more. *Amen*

New Every Morning

Ash Wednesday

O God, who desirest no sacrifice, but a humble and contrite spirit; and who wilt accept only such gifts as come from a good and honest heart: Save us, we pray thee, lest we come before thee with hands not free from stain; and mercifully accept the offerings of ourselves, who have nothing worthy to offer but what is from thee, and dare not offer what is not hallowed by thee; for Jesus Christ's sake. *Amen*

Daily Prayer

Most merciful Saviour,
you know what it is to be hungry and thirsty
for the will of the Father;
grant us your grace,
that in this service
we may know the forgiveness of our sins,
and always hunger and thirst
for your word of truth;
for your love's sake. *Amen*

C. N. R. Wallwork

Sixth Sunday before Easter

LENT 1

Blessed Jesu, lifting up holy hands perpetually for all mankind; Breathe by thy spirit such love into the prayers we offer, that they may be taken into thine, and prevail with thine; to the glory of thy name. *Amen*

Eric Milner-White

Heavenly Father, we thank you for giving your Son to die on the Cross that we might be forgiven. Help us to understand the extent of our sin and the greatness of his love, so that we may trust him as our Saviour and serve him as our Lord. *Amen*

M. H. Botting's collection

Fifth Sunday before Easter

LENT 2

O God, who art Light eternal; we beseech thee to shed the blessed beams of thy truth upon our understanding, that by instruction of thy word we may know thy will and be made wise unto salvation; through Jesus Christ our Lord. *Amen*

Book of Common Order

O Lord of heaven and earth:
bless the worship of your church in this place,
that we may hear your living Word,
through the power of the Holy Spirit. *Amen*

C. N. R. Wallwork

Fourth Sunday before Easter

LENT 3

O Lord, who for our sake didst endure the bitterness of death and despise the shame, and in thy cross and passion dost draw all men unto thyself: kindle in our hearts the vision of thy love, and shed abroad the light of thy victory in the darkness of the world; who now livest and reignest with the Father and the Holy Spirit, and art loved, worshipped, and adored, world without end. *Amen*

Frederick B. MacNutt

Lord Jesus Christ,
draw near to your people
from the throne of your heavenly glory;
that as we contemplate your bitter pain
upon the holy Cross,
we may be strengthened
by the proclamation of its life-giving mystery.
Amen

C. N. R. Wallwork

Third Sunday before Easter

LENT 4

O Spirit of the Highest, overshadow us with the bright cloud of thy presence, and speak to us out of the cloud; that while by faith we see Jesus wearing the robe of our nature made white and glistening, we may hear the voice out of the excellent glory: this is my beloved, my chosen, hear ye him. *Amen*

James Ferguson

Open our eyes, O God, to your glory, that we may worship in spirit and in truth, and offer you the praise of glad and thankful hearts. *Amen*

New Every Morning

Second Sunday before Easter

PASSION SUNDAY

Enable us, O Lord, to show how sweet it is to love thee, to bear with thee, to weep with thee, and for ever to rejoice with thee. *Amen*

Unknown
Sometimes attributed to Melanchthon

Lord of all power and might: assist the praises of your penitent and prayerful people, that we may worthily celebrate the mystery of your love and the triumphs of your grace; through Jesus Christ our Lord. *Amen*

C. N. R. Wallwork

The Sunday before Easter

PALM SUNDAY

O Lord Jesus Christ, who as on this day didst enter the rebellious city where thou wast to die; enter into our hearts, we beseech thee, and subdue them wholly to thyself. And as thy faithful disciples blessed thy coming, and spread their garments in the way, covering it with palm branches, make us ready to lay at thy feet all that we have and are, and to bless thee, O thou who comest in the name of the Lord. And grant that after having confessed and worshipped thee upon earth, we may be among the number of those who shall hail thine eternal triumph, and bear in their hands the palms of victory, when every knee shall bow before thee, and every tongue confess that thou art Lord, to the glory of God the Father. *Amen*

Book of Common Order

Lord Jesus Christ,
accept our songs of praise
as you journey to your Cross;
and enable us both to grieve at its necessity
and to be renewed by its power. *Amen*

C. N. R. Wallwork

Thursday before Easter

MAUNDY THURSDAY

O God, who by the blood of thy dear Son hast consecrated for us a new and living way into the holy place through the veil of his flesh; grant unto us the assurance of thy mercy, and sanctify us by thy heavenly grace, that we, approaching with pure heart and undefiled conscience, may offer unto thee a sacrifice in righteousness, and duly celebrate thy holy mysteries, to the glory of thy name; through Jesus Christ our Lord. *Amen*

W. E. Orchard
Adapted from Liturgy of Saint James

Most merciful Redeemer,
in the celebration of this memorial supper
you have bequeathed to your church
the eucharistic feast of your eternal sacrifice;
grant us faith to receive the grace
which you provide in this sacrament,
that we may eat at your royal banquet
with the saints in heaven. *Amen*

C. N. R. Wallwork

Good Friday

O God, our salvation and truth, grant that we thy children, rejecting the proud wisdoms of the world, may betake ourselves to the Cross of thy dear Son, to walk by its way, to repose in its shadow, to venerate its mercy, and to embrace its scorn: through the same Jesus Christ our Lord. *Amen*

Eric Milner-White

Almighty and eternal God, you raise us up and save us through the Passion of your Christ. As we celebrate this wonder, finish in us the work you have begun, and plant new zeal in our hearts through Jesus Christ, your Son, our Lord. *Amen*

Praise in All Our Days

Easter Day

EARLY COMMUNION

O Risen Lord, Son of the Father, who on the first day of the week didst open the eyes of Magdalen by speaking her name, and of wayfarers in the breaking of bread: Increase among this people the reverent esteem of thy holy day; that through the grace of thy Word and Sacraments, they may find thy presence in newness of life; who livest and reignest in the glory of the Eternal Trinity, world without end. *Amen*

Eric Milner-White

EARLY COMMUNION

God our Father, grant that as we joyfully celebrate the mysteries of the resurrection of our Lord Jesus Christ, so, in the world to come, we may, with all your saints, rejoice in the revelation of your glory; through him who loved us and washed us from our sins in his own blood, and who now lives and reigns with you and the holy Spirit, one God, always. *Amen*

Worship Now

Easter Day

O God, who by thine only-begotten Son hast overcome death, and opened unto us the gate of everlasting life; grant, we beseech thee, that those who have been redeemed by his passion may rejoice in his resurrection; through the same Christ our Lord. *Amen*

Gelasian Sacramentary

Be present, O Risen Lord,
in this your church's Easter praise;
that its anthems of joy
and its proclamation of your victory
may worthily celebrate
both the mystery of your redeeming love
and the majesty of your eternal glory.
Amen

C. N. R. Wallwork

The Sunday after Easter

O God, who makest us glad with the weekly remembrance of the glorious resurrection of thy Son our Lord; vouchsafe us this day such a blessing through thy worship, that the days which follow it may be spent in thy favour; through the same Jesus Christ our Lord. *Amen*

William Bright

Lord Jesus Christ, by your resurrection from the dead you have hallowed the first day of the week as a day of worship for your people: may we so die to sin and rise to newness of life that we may be worthy to offer up our prayers and praises on this and every day, to the honour and glory of your name. *Amen*

A Book of Common Prayer in Modern English

Second Sunday after Easter

Make our hearts to burn within us, O Christ, as we walk with thee in the way and listen to thy words; that we may go in the strength of thy presence and thy truth all our journey through, and at its end behold thee, in the glory of the Eternal Trinity, God for ever and ever. *Amen*

Eric Milner-White

Lord Jesus Christ, you are the Shepherd and we are your flock; protect us all, and save us from every danger; fulfil your promise and be with us at every moment, that we may come to bless your Name in the light of our resurrection, in your Kingdom which will have no end. *Amen*

Praise in All Our Days

Third Sunday after Easter

O Risen Lord, who after thy passion didst show thyself alive unto thine apostles by many infallible proofs, and didst speak unto them the things that concern the kingdom of God: speak unto us also who wait upon thee, and fill us with joy and peace in believing; that we may abound in hope, and knowing thy will may faithfully perform it, even unto the end; through thy grace, who livest and reignest, Lord of the dead and the living. *Amen*

Unknown

God our Father,
by raising Christ your Son
you conquered the power of death
and opened for us the way to eternal life.
Let our celebration today
raise us up and renew our lives
by the Spirit that is within us.
Grant this through our Lord Jesus Christ, your Son,
who lives and reigns with you and the Holy Spirit,
one God, for ever and ever. *Amen*

The Sunday Missal

Fourth Sunday after Easter

O Lord and Saviour, who art the way, the truth, and the life, reveal to us thy truth and inspire us with thy life, that, both now and at all times, we may find, in thee, the way to God; and this we ask for thy Name's sake. *Amen*

H. Bisseker

Lord, rule and guide your holy Church;
remain always her sole Shepherd, High Priest and Saviour;
give life and power to your Word,
and deepen our understanding of your redeeming mystery.
Amen

The Unity Book of Prayers

Fifth Sunday after Easter

Let thy mighty hand, O Lord God, and outstretched arm be our defence; thy mercy and loving-kindness in Jesus Christ, thy dear Son, our salvation; thy all-true word, our instruction; the grace of the life-giving Spirit, our comfort and consolation, unto the end and in the end; through the same Jesus Christ our Lord. *Amen*

Knox's Book of Common Order, 1564

Grant us, heavenly Father,
reverence, as we recall your glory,
understanding, as we recall your compassion,
and gratitude, as we recall your goodness;
so that we may go forth from this service
with our knowledge deepened,
with love rekindled,
and with strength to live better lives;
through Jesus Christ our Lord. *Amen*

Contemporary Parish Prayers

Ascension Day

O Christ, the King of Glory, who as on this day
didst mount in triumph unto thy royal estate:
Look favourably upon us, we humbly beseech thee,
that our devotion to the majesty of thy grace
may ascend to the throne of thy heavenly kingdom;
where thou livest and reignest with the Father
and the Holy Spirit, one God, world without end.
Amen

C. N. R. Wallwork

Lord Christ, holy and strong, holy and immortal:
God from God, Light from Light, born of a woman,
crucified, risen, ascended: receive our adoration,
our homage, and our love. ***Amen***

New Every Morning

Sixth Sunday after Easter

SUNDAY AFTER ASCENSION DAY

Almighty and eternal Father, who hast set thy Son Jesus upon the throne of thy kingdom, and hast crowned him with glory and honour: Bless, we beseech thee, this offering of our prayer and praise; that, through the intercession of Christ our great High Priest, we may render thee worship which is both acceptable and worthy; through the same Jesus Christ our Lord. *Amen*

C. N. R. Wallwork

Almighty God,
your Son ascended to the throne of power in heaven,
that he might be Lord over all things for his people:
We pray that the worship and service of the Church
may be inspired by his presence,
and that he will remain with us always,
to the end of the age. *Amen*

Collects with the New Lectionary

Pentecost

WHITSUNDAY

O God, the Father Almighty, who hast promised to give the Holy Spirit to them that ask thee: Look graciously upon us assembled with one accord in one place to make our prayer unto thee, and to wait for thy promise; and of thy abundant mercy renew in our longing hearts thy holy gift; through Jesus Christ our Lord. *Amen*

James Ferguson

O God, we pray that as the Holy Spirit came in wind and fire to the apostles, so he may come to us, breathing life into our souls and kindling in our hearts the flame of love; through Jesus Christ our Lord. *Amen*

J. W. G. Masterton

Trinity Sunday

FIRST SUNDAY AFTER PENTECOST

O Lord God Almighty, Eternal, Immortal, Invisible, the mysteries of whose being are unsearchable: accept, we beseech thee, our praises for the revelation which thou hast made of thyself, Father, Son, and Holy Spirit, three Persons, and one God; and mercifully grant, that ever holding fast this faith, we may magnify thy glorious name; who livest and reignest, one God, world without end. *Amen*

Bishop John Dowden

Eternal God,
you have shared with us
the mystery of your divine nature;
inspire, we pray, both our songs of praise
and the preaching of your word,
that we may rejoice in our Father's love
through the grace of our Lord Jesus Christ
in the fellowship of the Holy Spirit.
Amen

C. N. R. Wallwork

Second Sunday after Pentecost

TRINITY I

O Lord God Almighty, whose glory the Cherubim and Seraphim, and all the host of heaven, with ceaseless voice proclaim: we beseech thee to look graciously from thy dwelling-place upon us, thy humble servants, and in thy mercy vouchsafe to accept our unworthy prayers and praises; for the sake of our only Mediator and Advocate Jesus Christ our Lord. *Amen*

The Book of Common Prayer of the Scottish Church, 1912

Assist us, O God, with your Holy Spirit, that through our prayers and the proclamation of your Word, we may come, at last, to the heavenly joys which you have prepared for your people; through Jesus Christ our Lord. *Amen*

C. N. R. Wallwork

Third Sunday after Pentecost

TRINITY 2

Almighty God, without whose presence all worship is vain, and without whose light we have no understanding: vouchsafe to lead us into thy holy presence, and release us from the darkness of sin by thy heavenly light; that we, with all thy church, may worship thee this day in spirit and in truth, to the honour of thy name and the glory of thy kingdom; through Jesus Christ our Lord. *Amen*

The Book of Common Order, 1928

Lord Jesus Christ,
you are full of truth and grace;
reveal yourself in this your people's praise,
that we may know the truth
and bear witness to it by your grace.
Amen

C. N. R. Wallwork

Fourth Sunday after Pentecost

TRINITY 3

O most great and mighty God, whose glory is above all our thoughts and whose mercy is over all thy works: Let the inspiration of the Holy Spirit assist us in all the duties of this sacred day; let us join in the praise of thy church with ardent affection; let us hear thy Word with earnest attention and let the prayers and sacrifices of thy holy church offered unto thee this day, be graciously accepted. Being created by thee, let us ever act for thy glory, and being redeemed by thee, let us render unto thee what is thine; through Jesus Christ our Lord. *Amen*

John Wesley
Collection of Forms of Prayer, 1733

Most merciful God,
through your Son you have set us free
from slavery to sin,
that we might become your children;
help us in this our service of praise,
to sing of our freedom with joy,
to long for it in our prayers,
and to be assured of it in the proclamation
of your word;
through the same Jesus Christ our Lord.
Amen

C. N. R. Wallwork

Fifth Sunday after Pentecost

TRINITY 4

O God of hope, the true light of faithful souls, and perfect brightness of the blessed, who art verily the light of thy church, grant that our hearts may both render thee a worthy prayer, and always glorify thee with the offering of praises; through Jesus Christ our Lord. *Amen*

Gelasian Sacramentary

Most mighty God,
your power is as great as your love;
pour out your Spirit
upon your people,
that the power you give
both to our prayers and to our preaching
may enable us eternally to rejoice in your love;
through Jesus Christ our Lord.
Amen

C. N. R. Wallwork

Sixth Sunday after Pentecost

TRINITY 5

O God, the life of the faithful, the bliss of the righteous, mercifully receive the prayers of thy suppliants, that the souls which thirst for thy promises may evermore be filled from thine abundance; through Jesus Christ our Lord. *Amen*

Gelasian Sacramentary

O God, speak to us through your Word. Pour out upon us your grace that we may learn your will and obey your call; through Jesus Christ our Lord. *Amen*

F. W. Street

Seventh Sunday after Pentecost

TRINITY 6

Quicken, O God, our understanding and kindle our hearts, that we may be able to comprehend with all saints what is the breadth, and length, and depth, and height; and to know the love of Christ, which passeth knowledge, that we may be filled with all the fullness of God; through Jesus Christ our Lord. *Amen*

Book of Common Order, 1940

O Lord our God,
by your holy apostle
you have taught us
the abiding worth of your most excellent gifts;
be present in this the worship of your church,
that we may know the eternal faith
which gives us immortal hope
in your everlasting love;
through Jesus Christ our Lord.
Amen

C. N. R. Wallwork

Eighth Sunday after Pentecost

TRINITY 7

O Spirit of the living God, who dwellest in thy Church; who art holiness, wisdom and might; come thou, and fill the hearts of thy faithful people; and kindle within them the fire of thy love; through Jesus Christ our Lord.
Amen

Book of Common Order

May the Spirit of the Lord be upon us that we may announce good news to the poor, proclaim release for the prisoners, and recovery of sight for the blind; that we may let the broken victim go free, and proclaim the year of the Lord's favour; according to the example of Christ and by his grace.
Amen

Prayers for Today's Church

Ninth Sunday after Pentecost

TRINITY 8

Grant, O Lord, that all who worship within this place may present their bodies a living sacrifice, holy, acceptable unto thee; and that they may themselves be temples of the Holy Spirit wherein thou wilt dwell for evermore. *Amen*

The Book of Worship

Lord our God, help us to give our minds to you in our worship, so that we may listen to what you have to say to us, and know your will.
Help us to give our hearts to you in our worship, so that we may really want to do what you require from us.
Help us to give our strength to you in our worship, so that through us your will may be done.
In the name of Jesus Christ our Lord. *Amen*

Contemporary Prayers for Church and School

Tenth Sunday after Pentecost

TRINITY 9

Awaken us fully to thy presence, O God, that we may bow before thee with reverence, praise thee with joy, and serve thee with love; through Jesus Christ our Lord. *Amen*

J. W. G. Masterton

Almighty God, your glory was manifested in the Cross of our Lord Jesus Christ; may the contemplation of this love fill us with joy and hope, for he lives and reigns now and for ever. *Amen*

Praise in All Our Days

Eleventh Sunday after Pentecost

TRINITY 10

Go before us, O Lord, in all our doings with thy most gracious favour, and further us with thy continual help; that in all our works, begun, continued, and ended in thee, we may glorify thy holy name, and finally by thy mercy obtain everlasting life; through Jesus Christ our Lord. *Amen*

Gregorian Sacramentary

Holy Spirit of God, source of knowledge
and creator of fellowship:
open our minds to recognize the truth
and our hearts to welcome it,
that in company together we may learn your will
and be strengthened to obey it;
through Jesus Christ our Lord. *Amen*

Basil Naylor

Twelfth Sunday after Pentecost

TRINITY 11

Grant, O Lord, that thy holy Word, which shall be read and preached in this place, may be grafted inwardly in the hearts of those who hear, so that they may both perceive and know what things they ought to do, and also may have grace and power faithfully to fulfil the same; through Jesus Christ our Lord. *Amen*

Services for Use in the Diocese of Southwark

O Lord our God,
bless and sanctify
this our offering of prayer and praise,
that under the gracious ministry of your holy Word
we may be refreshed and strengthened
for the work which you have given us to do;
through Jesus Christ our Lord.
Amen

C. N. R. Wallwork

Thirteenth Sunday after Pentecost

TRINITY 12

Grant us, we beseech thee, O Lord, the aid of thy Holy Spirit, that, whatever by his teaching we know to be our duty, we may by his grace be enabled to perform; through Jesus Christ our Lord. *Amen*

J. C. Chute

Most holy God,
your majesty is exceeded
only by your love;
grant us, in this our worship of you,
penitence in the presence of your holiness,
reverence at the thought of your majesty,
and confidence in the knowledge of your love;
through Jesus Christ our Lord.
Amen

C. N. R. Wallwork

Fourteenth Sunday after Pentecost

TRINITY 13

O God, eternal and ever blessed, who callest us to worship thee in spirit and in truth; look mercifully upon us as we worship and adore thee. Order what is disordered in our lives, bring our minds to thy truth, our conscience to thy law, and our hearts to thy love; that, in fellowship with all thy church, we may hear thy voice and be enabled to answer thee with humble trust and willing obedience; through Jesus Christ our Lord. *Amen*

Prayers for the Christian Year

Lamb of God,
you are worthy to receive
the blessings of all the heavenly host;
look upon our worship
with the bright beams of your everlasting mercy,
that through this our celebration
of your glorious gospel
we may share the splendour of your eternal kingdom.
Amen

C. N. R. Wallwork

Fifteenth Sunday after Pentecost

TRINITY 14

O God, before whose throne the whole family of heaven and earth bow down in ceaseless adoration: Accept, we pray thee, the praises which we offer thee this day. Make us to know the joy of thy salvation, that with glad hearts we may proclaim thy Word in such wise that the sorrowing may be comforted, the faint in heart made strong, the wayward restored to ways of life and peace, and thy saving health be made known to all nations; through Jesus Christ our Lord. *Amen*

Fred D. Gealey

Most gracious God,
your glory is the only purpose of our worship;
accept your people's praise,
inspire our prayers,
and speak to us in the preaching of your Word;
through Jesus Christ our Lord.
Amen

C. N. R. Wallwork

Sixteenth Sunday after Pentecost

TRINITY 15

O loving Lord, be near us in this time of worship. Open our ears to hear thy voice; open our eyes to behold thy glory; open our hearts to receive thy grace; open our lips to show forth thy praise; for the sake of Jesus Christ our Saviour.
Amen

Frank Colquhoun

Eternal God,
you are surrounded by the light of heavenly splendour;
grant us so to celebrate
the truth of your gospel
that we may see your glory
in the face of Jesus Christ.
Amen

C. N. R. Wallwork

Seventeenth Sunday after Pentecost

TRINITY 16

O God of peace, who hast taught us that in returning and rest we shall be saved, in quietness and confidence shall be our strength: By the might of thy Spirit, lift us, we pray thee, to thy presence, where we may be still and know that thou art God; through Jesus Christ our Lord. *Amen*

The Book of Worship

O Lord our God, in whose word we are commanded to seek your presence; aid us in both our prayers and our praises, that the grace which we desire by faith we may accept with joy, to the glory of your precious name; through Jesus Christ our Lord. *Amen*

C. N. R. Wallwork

Eighteenth Sunday after Pentecost

TRINITY 17

O living Christ, make us conscious now of thy healing nearness. Touch our eyes that we may see thee; open our ears that we may hear thy voice; enter our hearts that we may know thy love. Overshadow our souls and bodies with thy presence, that we may partake of thy strength, thy love and thy healing life; through the same Christ our Lord. *Amen*

Howard Chandler Robbins

O God, empower us for what is waiting to be done, guide us in the doing of it, and uphold us until it is completed. And in it all may there be honour and glory to you, through Jesus Christ our Lord. *Amen*

Worship Now

Nineteenth Sunday after Pentecost

TRINITY 18

O Lord, heavenly Father, in whom is the fulness of light and of wisdom; enlighten our minds by the Holy Spirit, and give us grace to receive thy Word with reverence and humility, without which no man can understand thy truth; for Christ's sake. *Amen*

John Calvin

Father,
help us in this act of worship
to celebrate the majesty of your glory,
to proclaim the victory of Christ's cross,
and to rejoice in the power of the Holy Spirit,
for your love's sake.
Amen

C. N. R. Wallwork

Twentieth Sunday after Pentecost

TRINITY 19

Lord, make us, we beseech thee, like-minded with all saints whether on earth or in heaven; that we may worship thee as they worship, trust as they trust, rejoice in thee as they rejoice, love thee as they love; for the sake of our Saviour Jesus Christ. *Amen*

Christina Rossetti

Eternal God and Father, Lord of our lives,
forgive all that hinders our communion with you
and with one another;
that our worship may be in the fellowship of the Spirit
and in the name of your Son,
Jesus Christ our Lord. *Amen*

Basil Naylor

Twenty-first Sunday after Pentecost

TRINITY 20

Grant, O God most merciful, that thee whom we confess with all our mind, we may worship with all our strength, and love with all our soul; and so confessing, worshipping and loving, we may come to behold thee in thy celestial glory; through Jesus Christ our Lord. *Amen*

Eric Milner-White

Lord, teach us to pray.
Help us to come with boldness to the throne of grace.
Make us conscious of your presence in our midst.
Give us the freedom of the Holy Spirit.
Enlarge our vision and increase our faith.
And may our words and our thoughts be now acceptable in your sight,
O Lord, our rock and our redeemer. *Amen*

Frank Colquhoun

Twenty-second Sunday after Pentecost

TRINITY 21

O God, in whom we live and move and have our being,
by thy Spirit help us to worship thee.
Assured of thy love and mercy,
may we come humbly to thy throne of grace.
Hungry and thirsty,
may we find thy Word meat and drink to our souls.
Eager to know and serve thee,
may we see thy face in Jesus Christ our Lord,
and learn from him the way of life. *Amen*

R. W. Stewart

God of glory,
you have made us to share through Christ
the mystery of worship with the host of heaven and all creation:
Give us reality in our worship,
that we may acknowledge you in reverence and sincerity
and work for justice and freedom among all men;
through Jesus Christ our Lord. *Amen*

Collects with the New Lectionary

Twenty-third Sunday after Pentecost

TRINITY 22

O Eternal God, who hast called us to be a holy priesthood, to offer spiritual sacrifices: grant to us now the aid of thy Holy Spirit, that our praises and prayers, our offerings and the oblation of our lives, may be acceptable unto thee; through Jesus Christ our Lord. *Amen*

Orders and Prayers for Church Worship

Almighty God and Father, help us to be still in your presence, that we may know ourselves to be your people, and you to be our God; through Jesus Christ our Lord. *Amen*

New Every Morning

*All Saints' Day**

NOVEMBER 1st

Almighty and everlasting God, who dost enkindle the flame of thy love in the hearts of the Saints, grant to our minds the same faith and power of love; that as we rejoice in their triumphs, we may profit by their examples; through Jesus Christ our Lord. *Amen*

Gothic Missal

Almighty God, break the power of darkness, let your glory appear among us and make us sharers of your eternity, with all your saints, through Jesus Christ our Lord. *Amen*

Praise in All Our Days

* When this falls on a Sunday these prayers replace those of the ordinary Sunday of the calendar.

Part Two

PRAYERS FOR SPECIAL OCCASIONS

A Saint's Day or a Memorial Service

O Lord Jesus Christ, the hope of the martyrs and the joy of the saints, who hast called thy church into the bright succession of the apostles and evangelists: Assure us this day of their fellowship, and grant that having worshipped thee here on earth, we may attain at length unto the company of those who continually bless thee in heaven; for thy name's sake. *Amen*

C. N. R. Wallwork

Almighty God, from whose love in Christ
we cannot be parted, by death or by life:
hear our prayers and thanksgivings
for those whom we remember this day.
Fulfil in them the purpose of your love;
and bring us, with them, to your eternal joy;
through Jesus Christ our Lord. *Amen*

Contemporary Parish Prayers

Renewal of the Covenant

O holy and merciful God, our heavenly Father, who hast taught us that upon our present choice depends our eternal lot: Accept, we beseech thee, the worship of thy penitent servants, and grant that with humble confession and holy vow we may renew our express and solemn covenant with thee; through Jesus Christ our Lord. *Amen*

Nineteenth-century Methodist Covenant Service

God of peace,
you call men to repentance
and have graciously met their needs in a new covenant:
Give us true penitence for our sin,
Enable us to fulfil the ministry you set before us,
Make us holy in every part of our being;
Through Jesus Christ our Lord. *Amen*

Collects with the New Lectionary

Week of Prayer for Christian Unity

In thy house, O Lord, let us dwell in peace and concord; give us all one heart, one mind, one true interpretation upon thy word; that all who believe in thee may together extol thy name; O Lord God, most glorious and excellent over all. *Amen*

Godly Prayers, 1552

Lord our God, giver of all grace, have mercy on your Church throughout the world.
Renew its life;
restore its unity;
sanctify its worship;
empower its witness;
and make it a fit instrument for the furtherance
of Christ's kingdom among men, to the glory of his great name. *Amen*

Frank Colquhoun

Aldersgate Sunday or the Conversion of John Wesley

Almighty God, from whose free and universal grace we receive both the assurance of faith and the holiness of perfect love: Bless, we beseech thee, both our ministry of praise and the proclamation of thy gospel, that the Church of Jesus may bring forth her increase to thy glory; through the same Jesus Christ thy Son our Lord, who liveth and reigneth with thee and the Holy Spirit, ever one God, world without end. *Amen*

C. N. R. Wallwork

The crowning glory of your goodness, Lord, is that you have assured us of your continuing love and grace. Through this divine service assure us that our sins are forgiven, hope is rekindled and power offered to us to live more nearly as we pray. Help us now in faith, hope and love to share in this worship to your honour and glory; through Jesus Christ out Lord. *Amen*

The Divine Service

First Sunday of the Methodist Connexional Year

Almighty and everlasting God, creator of the whole universe, who hast appointed times by thine own power: Bless this our offering of prayer and praise; and of thy goodness, O Lord, preserve thy faithful people with the hand of thy perpetual providence; through Jesus Christ our Lord. *Amen*

Based on an Eastern Orthodox prayer for the beginning of the Church's Year

Eternal God, help us to remember your presence with us now as we lead the worship of your people; and may their hearts and ours be lifted up in humble prayer and joyful praise, to the glory of our Lord Jesus Christ. *Amen*

Contemporary Parish Prayers

Harvest Thanksgiving

O Almighty and everlasting God, who hast given unto us the fruits of the earth in their season, and hast crowned the year with thy goodness: Give us grateful hearts, that we may unfeignedly thank thee for all thy loving-kindness, and worthily magnify thy holy Name; through Jesus Christ our Lord. *Amen*

Bishop John Dowden

O Lord, whose mercy reaches to the heavens, whose faithfulness knows no end: let the greatness of your love be known to us, that we may worship you with wonder, joy and thanksgiving. *Amen*

New Every Morning

Education Sunday

O heavenly King, the Comforter, thou Spirit of truth who art everywhere present and fillest all things, the treasury of blessings and giver of life: Cleanse us from every stain, and come, take up thine abode within us, O thou strength of our souls and our salvation for ever. *Amen*

Liturgy of Saint John Chrysostom

You came, Lord Jesus Christ,
to teach us the way of life which God requires:
Make us receptive to your word,
and help us to obey, whatever it may cost,
that our lives may bear much fruit;
To the glory of your name. *Amen*

Collects with the New Lectionary

Remembrance Sunday

O God, our Refuge and Strength, and our most mighty Deliverer, by whose mercy we are spared, by whose providence we are governed, and by whose love we have been redeemed: grant us the help of thy Holy Spirit, that we may praise thee for thy goodness and do all things to thy glory, and that our worship may be acceptable to thee; through Jesus Christ our Lord. *Amen*

James M. Todd

Eternal Word of the Father: for our salvation you became one with us in everything but sin. Give us the light of your liberating word. May we not only hear it, but act upon it; and so lead us into God's kingdom where you live and reign for ever. *Amen*

Praise in All Our Days

Christian Citizenship Sunday

O Lord, go thou with us into thy holy place, and let thy Spirit guide our worship. May souls be turned to thee, here and everywhere, through the reading and preaching of thy Word. Keep us from presumptuous sins, from fear of men and surrender to evil. And be thou evermore our guide, our light, our comfort; for Jesus' sake. *Amen*

Book of Common Order

Lord God, may your eternal light and your enduring truth lead us to your presence. Speak with living voice to our hearts: speak, and let your servants hear. May your Spirit among us enable us to make good use of the liberty you give us; through Jesus Christ our Lord. *Amen*

Contemporary Prayers for Church and School

Watchnight Service

O Lord, our God, in thy Son our Lord Jesus Christ, thou hast made us thy children. We have heard thy call and come now to praise thee, to hear thy Word, and to call to thee. Be thou thyself in our midst, so that this may be an hour of light, in which we see heaven opened and then a little brightness on this dark earth; through Jesus Christ our Lord. *Amen*

Karl Barth

Lord Jesus,
you asked your disciples to watch with you
for one brief hour of prayer.
Bless our midnight songs of praise,
that in these solemn moments
we may know your presence
and be awake to your glory.
Amen

C. N. R. Wallwork

Church Anniversary

O Almighty Father, who art adored by thy holy angels, and yet art pleased to accept the praises of sinful men: Let thy glory fill this house of prayer, we beseech thee; and mercifully grant that all who worship thee here may be numbered at the last with those who sing the new song before thy heavenly throne; through Jesus Christ our Lord, who livest and reignest with thee and the Holy Spirit, ever one God, world without end. *Amen*

Parish Prayers

Father,
each year we recall the dedication of this church
to your service.
Let our worship always be sincere
and help us to find your saving love in this church.
Grant this through our Lord Jesus Christ, your Son,
who lives and reigns with you and the Holy Spirit,
one God, for ever and ever. *Amen*

The Sunday Missal

Sunday School Anniversary

O God, our heavenly Father, who lovest all thy children and forgettest none; accept us as we come to thee with humble and reverent hearts, and be pleased to pour out thy blessing upon us; through Jesus Christ our Lord. *Amen*

Book of Common Order

Father, as we now prepare to share in the activity of worship cleanse our hearts and minds, fill us with your Holy Spirit, and open our lips to show forth your praise; for the sake of Jesus Christ our Lord. *Amen*

Contemporary Parish Prayers

Choir Sunday

O Lord God Almighty, whose glory Cherubim and Seraphim and all the hosts of heaven with ceaseless voice proclaim: Hear and accept, we humbly beseech thee, the praises of thy Church below; and pour down upon thy ministers in choir and sanctuary such a spirit of faith, reverence, and joy as shall lift both their hymns and their lives unto thee; through Jesus Christ our Lord. *Amen*

Eric Milner-White

Bless, O God, those who sing in the choir of this church, that with heart and voice they may make melody to the Lord; and may they so lead our praises that together we may magnify your glorious name, through Jesus Christ our Lord. *Amen*

Frank Colquhoun

Men's Sunday

Bless all who worship thee,
from the rising of the sun unto the going down of the same.
Of thy goodness, give us;
with thy love, inspire us;
by thy Spirit, guide us;
by thy power, protect us;
in thy mercy, receive us now and always.
Amen

Divinc Worship

Almighty God,
your Son has opened for us
a new and living way into your presence:
Give us pure hearts and obedient wills,
That we may worship you in spirit and in truth;
Through Jesus Christ our Lord. *Amen*

Collects with the New Lectionary

Women's Sunday

Almighty God and Father, whose risen Son first appeared to Mary, that she might announce her news with joy: Pour out upon us, we beseech thee, thy Holy Spirit, that this our offering of Divine praise may worthily set forth the glorious mystery of our redemption; through the same Jesus Christ, thy Son our Lord. *Amen*

C. N. R. Wallwork

O God our Father,
Your beloved Son's Mother is praised above all women
for her obedience and devotion to your Word;
overshadow this our worship,
with your most Holy Spirit;
that we may be obedient to that same Word
and devoted always to your will. *Amen*

C. N. R. Wallwork

Overseas Missions Sunday

Eternal Father, of whom the whole family in heaven and earth is named: Unite us, as we worship thee here, with all who in far-off places are lifting up their hands and hearts to thee; that thy church throughout the world, with the church in heaven, may offer up one sacrifice of thanksgiving; to the praise and honour of thy holy name. *Amen*

Eric Milner-White and G. W. Briggs

Creator of the universe, watch over us and keep us in the light of your presence. May our praise continually blend with that of all creation, until we come together to the eternal joys which you promise in your love, through Jesus Christ our Lord. *Amen*

Praise in All Our Days

Home Missions Sunday

Almighty God, who hast made the Church thy dwelling place; be pleased to manifest thyself to us thy servants who meet this day in thy holy place; and inspire our hearts to worship thee in spirit and in truth; through Jesus Christ our Lord. *Amen*

Ordinal and Service Book

Send forth your Spirit, Lord,
And renew the face of the earth.
May the grace of the Holy Spirit bless us
and may the Lord be with us. *Amen*

The Unity Book of Prayers

Circuit Rally

O Almighty and everlasting God, who didst give to thine Apostles grace truly to believe and to preach thy Word; grant, we beseech thee, unto thy Church to love the Word which they believed, and both to preach and receive the same: through Jesus Christ thy Son our Lord, who liveth and reigneth with thee in the unity of the Holy Spirit, ever one God, world without end. *Amen*

The Prayer Book Revised: English Church Union, 1923

Eternal Lord God, as is your majesty
so is your mercy.
Open our eyes to your light,
our hearts to your love,
and our minds to your truth,
that we may praise you now and always,
through Jesus Christ our Lord. *Amen*

New Every Morning

Youth Sunday

Almighty God, we invoke thee, the fountain of everlasting light, and entreat thee to send forth thy truth into our hearts, and to pour upon us the glory of thy brightness; through Jesus Christ our Lord. *Amen*

The Book of Worship

Heavenly Father,
you have revealed yourself to us
in the mystery of the gospel of Christ;
pour upon us your Holy Spirit,
that in this our worship of you
we may share in the good news of your kingdom
and praise you for its fellowship;
through the same Christ our Lord. *Amen*

C. N. R. Wallwork

Local Preachers' Sunday

O Lord Jesus Christ, who by thy glorious resurrection hast sanctified a day of rest for thy people: Grant that we, dying unto sin and rising again to newness of life, may worthily offer up our prayers and praises to thy honour and glory; who livest and reignest with the Father and the Holy Spirit, one God, world without end. *Amen*

Traditional in York Minster

O God, source of light and of life, you have led us out of darkness into your marvellous light, from death into life and from slavery to freedom through the resurrection of your only Son. Lighten our hearts by the brightness of your Holy Spirit. Sanctify us entirely, body, mind and soul, in the communion of all the saints, through Christ our Lord. *Amen*

Praise in All Our Days

The Recognition and Commissioning of a Local Preacher

Almighty God, without whom we can do no good thing;
grant us now the aid of thy divine grace, that the prayers
which we offer and the vows which are taken before thee
may be acceptable unto thee;
through Jesus Christ our Lord. *Amen*

Ordinal and Service Book

Lord God,
we are taught in Scripture
that the people shall not hear without a preacher:
Pour out your Spirit upon your gospel church
in this place,
that the prayers and promises of this day
may be found worthy in your sight;
through Jesus Christ our Lord. *Amen*

C. N. R. Wallwork

Holy Baptism

Almighty and everlasting God, whose blessed Son, Jesus Christ our Lord, hath ordained this holy Sacrament; mercifully look upon us, we beseech thee, who are met together in his name, and ratify in heaven that which, by his appointment, we do upon earth; through the same Jesus Christ our Lord. *Amen*

Book of Common Order

God our Father,
in your Son you have commanded us to baptise all nations:
Accept those whom we baptise in this sacrament,
and grant that they may be united to Christ in his church
and receive, according to his promise,
the forgiveness of sins
and the gift of the Holy Spirit;
through the same Christ our Lord. *Amen*

C. N. R. Wallwork

The Confirmation of Church Members

O God of all goodness and grace, whose beloved Son hath promised the Comforter to his disciples: Prepare our hearts and minds, we beseech thee, so to approach this holy ordinance, that thy penitent and faithful servants may be strengthened with the power and gifts of the Holy Spirit; through the same Jesus Christ, thy Son our Lord. *Amen*

C. N. R. Wallwork

O Lord our God,
give your people grace to hear and receive your word,
and to bring forth the fruit of the Spirit;
through Jesus Christ our Lord. *Amen*

The Litany, 1975

The Welcome of New Ministers

O Lord Jesus Christ, our good High Priest and our most merciful Redeemer, who hast bestowed upon thy Church the manifold gifts of thy grace: Bless, we beseech thee, the ministry both of our proclamation and our praise, that we may attain at length unto the fellowship of thine eternal kingdom. *Amen*

C. N. R. Wallwork

Eternal Father,
the triumphs of your Son
are sung eternally in heaven;
by the power of your Spirit
bless the word of Christ's victory
and guide our joyful response,
that our hymns of praise may be one
with the songs of the saints in light;
through the same Jesus Christ our Lord.
Amen

C. N. R. Wallwork

Acknowledgements

THE Compiler wishes to express his thanks to the following for permission to reproduce prayers of which they are the authors, publishers, or copyright owners.

In a few instances it has not been possible to trace ownership. If there has been any infringement of copyright it is hoped that this will be pardoned.

The Church of Melanesia and Father Brian MacDonald-Milne for a prayer from *A Book of Common Prayer in Modern English.*

James Clark & Co. Ltd for prayers from *Prayers for Common Worship* by James Ferguson (originally published by Allenson & Co. Ltd).

The Revd Stephen F. Winward for a prayer from *Orders and Prayers for Church Worship* compiled by Ernest A. Payne and Stephen F. Winward and published by the Baptist Union.

The Revd James M. Todd for prayers from *New Every Morning* (New Edition, 1973) published by the BBC and for a prayer from *A Book of Services and Prayers* published by The Independent Press.

The Saint Andrew Press for prayers from *Prayers for Use in Church* by J. W. G. Masterton and for prayers from *Worship Now* compiled by D. Cairns and others.

S.C.M. Press Ltd and William B. Eerdmans Publishing Co. for prayers from *Contemporary Prayers for Public Worship* and *Contemporary Prayers for Church and School* edited by Caryl Micklem.

Oxford University Press for prayers from *Daily Prayer* by Eric Milner-White and G. W. Briggs.

The Committee on Public Worship and Aids to Devotion of the Church of Scotland for a prayer from the *Book of Common Order 1928*, for prayers from *The Book of Common Order 1940*, for a prayer from *The Ordinal and Service Book* (2nd Edition, 1954), for a prayer from *Prayers for the Christian Year* (2nd Edition, 1952) and for a prayer from *The Divine Service* (1973).

The Methodist Church Division of Education and Youth for a prayer from *Together in Church* published by the Methodist Youth Department.

The Church Pastoral Aid Society for prayers from *Prayers for Today's Church* edited by Dick Williams.

The Faith Press for prayers from *Praise in All Our Days* originally published in French by Les Presses de Taizé, Taizé-Communauté.

I.C.E.L. for the English translation of prayers from the *Roman Missal*; Copyright © 1973, International Committee on English in the Liturgy, Inc. All rights reserved.

Collins Publishers for prayers from *The Minister's Prayer Book* by John W. Doberstein.

Canon Frank Colquhoun for a prayer from *New Every Morning* (New Edition, 1973) published by the BBC.

Geoffrey Chapman Publishers for prayers from *The Unity Book of Prayers* originally published in French by Les Editions du Cerf under the title *Le livre de l'unité* and for prayers from *A Christian's Prayer Book* by Peter Coughlan, Ronald C. D. Jasper and Teresa Rodrigues, O.S.B.

Grove Books for prayers from *Collects with the New Lectionary* by Peter R. Akehurst and Anthony J. Bishop.

Longman Group Limited for prayers from *A Cambridge Bede Book* by Eric Milner-White and for a prayer from *Prayers for the City of God* by G. C. Binyon.

Cambridge University Press and the Publications Committee of the Episcopal Church in Scotland for a prayer from the *Book of Common Prayer for Scotland* (1912) and for prayers from the *Scottish Book of Common Prayer 1929*.

A. R. Mowbray & Co. Ltd for prayers from *After the Third Collect* by Eric Milner-White and for prayers from *The Prayer Manual* by Frederick B. Macnutt.

S.P.C.K. for prayers from *A Procession of Passion Prayers* by Eric Milner-White, for a prayer from *A Manual of Eastern Orthodox Prayers* published for The Fellowship of St Alban and St Sergius, for a prayer from *Services for Use in the Diocese of Southwark* and for a petition from *Morning and Evening Prayer Alternative Services Series 3*, copyright The Registrars of the Provinces of Canterbury and York.

Hodder & Stoughton Limited for prayers from *Parish Prayers* and *Contemporary Parish Prayers* by Frank Colquhoun.

The United Methodist Publishing House (U.S.A.) for prayers from the *Book of Worship*, Copyright © 1964, 1965 by the Board of Publication of the Methodist Church, Inc.

Extracts from the *Book of Common Prayer* of 1662, which is Crown Copyright, are used with permission.

Sources of Prayers

1. The source in the left-hand column refers to the first prayer on each page and that in the right-hand column to the second.
2. The figures after each code refer to the page number in that particular book.

Sundays before Christmas

9th	DP 12	CPP 31
8th	LS	SM 372
7th	JT	NEM 9
6th	DP 114	TC 45
5th	DP 163	NEM 97
4th	BW 129	NEM 2
3rd	EB	PTC No. 8
2nd	PP 150	CNL 35
Last	BAC 27	CPB 335

Christmas Eve

	VP	VP

Christmas Day

	BAC 23	CPB 70

Sundays after Christmas

1st	BAC 28	CPP 29
2nd	DP 58	UP 41

Epiphany

	PPP 3	VP

Sundays after Epiphany

1st	DP 22	CPB 84
2nd	DP 25	CPPW 63
3rd	BCP Epiphany 1	CPPW 17
4th	PCG 83	VP
5th	MPB 138	VP
6th	BW 169	NEM 118

Sundays before Easter

9th	CB 127	SP 119
8th	BAC 65	VP
7th	PM 80	NEM 79

Ash Wednesday

	DP 116	VP

Sundays before Easter (continued)

6th	CB 133	PTC No. 96
5th	BCO (1940) 48	VP
4th	PM 110	VP
3rd	PCW 352	NEM 5
2nd	MPB 142	VP

Palm Sunday

	BCO (1940) 242	VP

Maundy Thursday

	DS 122	VP

Good Friday

	PPP 4	PAD 133

Easter Day: Early Communion

	CB 103	WN 168

Easter Day

	GS	VP

Sundays after Easter

1st	BAC 233	BCPM 58
2nd	CB 93	PAD 200
3rd	PM 113	SM 240
4th	BPS 274	UP 87
5th	BCO (1564)	CPP 108

Ascension Day

	VP	NEM 21

Sunday after Ascension

	VP	CNL 21

Pentecost

	PCW 203	PUC 77

Trinity Sunday

	SBCP 349	VP

Sundays after Pentecost

2nd	BCPS 52	VP
3rd	BCO (1928) 193	VP
4th	CFP 24	VP
5th	BAC 4	VP
6th	BAC 4	PTC No. 429
7th	BCO (1940) 137	VP
8th	BCO (1940) 73	PTC No. 130
9th	BW 170	CPCS 11
10th	PUC 45	PAD 249
11th	BCP P.Com. (4)	CPP 207
12th	SS 48	VP
13th	DP 54	VP
14th	PCY 63	VP
15th	BW 167	VP
16th	PP 351	VP
17th	BW 166	VP
18th	DG 223	WN 185
19th	PP 415	VP
20th	DP 115	CPP 106
21st	CB 91	CPP 105
22nd	BSP 128	CNL 29
23rd	OP 62	NEM 93

All Saints' Day

	BAC 69	PAD 309

A Saint's Day or Memorial Service

	VP	CPP 78

Renewal of the Covenant

	VP	CNL 29

Week of Prayer for Christian Unity

	DP 111	CPP 174

Aldersgate Sunday

	VP	TDS 30

1st Sunday of Methodist Year

	MOP 45	CPP 234

Harvest Thanksgiving

	SBCP 293	NEM 13

Education Sunday

	SJC	CNL 15

Remembrance Sunday

	BSP 228	PAD 235

Christian Citizenship Sunday
BCO (1940) 3 CPCS 9

Watchnight Service
SPB 60 VP

Church Anniversary
PP 177 SM 777

Sunday School Anniversary
BCO (1940) 75 CPP 234

Choir Sunday
ATC 35 CPP 213

Men's Sunday
DW 30 CNL 15

Women's Sunday
VP VP

Overseas Missions Sunday
DP 68 PAD 196

Home Missions Sunday
OSB 9 UP 95

Circuit Rally
PB (1923) 324 NEM 71

Youth Sunday
BW 76 VP

Local Preachers' Sunday
ATC 112 PAD 184

Recognition and Commissioning of Local Preachers
OSB 2 VP

Holy Baptism
BCO (1940) 97 VP

Confirmation of Church Members
VP MEP 48

Welcome of New Ministers
VP VP

Code to Sources of Prayers

ATC	AFTER THE THIRD COLLECT Eric Milner-White A. R. Mowbray and Co. Ltd 1952
BAC	ANCIENT COLLECTS William Bright Oxford: James Parker & Co. 1861 (7th Edition 1902)
BCO (1564)	BOOK OF COMMON ORDER John Knox 1564
BCO (1928)	BOOK OF COMMON ORDER United Free Church of Scotland Oxford University Press 1928
BCO (1940)	BOOK OF COMMON ORDER Church of Scotland Oxford University Press 1940
BCP	BOOK OF COMMON PRAYER 1662
BCPM	A BOOK OF COMMON PRAYER IN MODERN ENGLISH Diocese of Melanesia Press
BCPS	BOOK OF COMMON PRAYER OF THE SCOTTISH CHURCH Edinburgh: Cambridge University Press 1912
BPS	A BOOK OF PRAYERS FOR SCHOOLS S.C.M. Press 1936
BSP	A BOOK OF SERVICES AND PRAYERS Independent Press Ltd 1959
BW	THE BOOK OF WORSHIP The United Methodist Church Nashville, Tennessee 1964 and 1965
CB	A CAMBRIDGE BEDE BOOK Eric Milner-White Longman, Green & Co. 1936
CFP	A COLLECTION OF FORMS OF PRAYER John Wesley 1733 Editor F. C. Gill: Epworth Press 1951
CNL	COLLECTS WITH THE NEW LECTIONARY Akehurst and Bishop Grove Books 1972 and 1973
CPB	A CHRISTIAN'S PRAYER BOOK Coughlan, Jasper and Rodrigues Geoffrey Chapman 1973
CPCS	CONTEMPORARY PRAYERS FOR CHURCH AND SCHOOL Editor Caryl Micklem: S.C.M. Press Ltd 1975
CPP	CONTEMPORARY PARISH PRAYERS Frank Colquhoun Hodder and Stoughton 1975
CPPW	CONTEMPORARY PRAYERS FOR PUBLIC WORSHIP Editor Caryl Micklem: S.C.M. Press Ltd 1967

DG	A DIARY OF PRAYER Elizabeth Goudge Hodder and Stoughton 1966
DP	DAILY PRAYER Eric Milner-White and G. W. Briggs Oxford University Press 1941
DS	DIVINE SERVICE W. E. Orchard Oxford University Press 1919
DW	DIVINE WORSHIP Methodist Publishing House 1935
EB	EXPOSITORS' BIBLE, Isaiah: George Adam Smith London 1890 and 1927
GS	GELASIAN SACRAMENTARY
JT	JEREMY TAYLOR
LS	LEONINE SACRAMENTARY
MEP	MORNING AND EVENING PRAYER Alternative Services Series 3 The Registrars of the Provinces of Canterbury and York London 1974 and 1975
MOP	A MANUAL OF EASTERN ORTHODOX PRAYERS S.P.C.K. 1945
MPB	THE MINISTER'S PRAYER BOOK Editor John W. Doberstein Collins 1964
NEM	NEW EVERY MORNING, New Edition, BBC London 1973
OP	ORDERS AND PRAYERS FOR CHURCH WORSHIP Ernest A. Payne and Stephen F. Winward Baptist Union 1960 and 1965
OSB	ORDINAL AND SERVICE BOOK For use in the Courts of the Church of Scotland Oxford University Press 1931 and 1954
PAD	PRAISE IN ALL OUR DAYS Common Prayer at Taizé Faith Press 1975
PB (1923)	THE PRAYER BOOK REVISED The English Church Union Oxford University Press 1923
PCG	PRAYERS FOR THE CITY OF GOD G. C. Binyon Longmans, Green & Co.
PCW	PRAYERS FOR COMMON WORSHIP James Ferguson Allenson & Co. Ltd 1936
PCY	PRAYERS FOR THE CHRISTIAN YEAR Church of Scotland Oxford University Press 1952 Second Edition
PM	THE PRAYER MANUAL F. B. McNutt A. R. Mowbray & Co. Ltd 1959
PP	PARISH PRAYERS Frank Colquhoun Hodder and Stoughton 1967
PPP	A PROCESSION OF PASSION PRAYERS Eric Milne-White S.P.C.K. 1962

PTC	PRAYERS FOR TODAY'S CHURCH Editor R. H. C. Williams C.P.A.S. Publications London 1972
PUC	PRAYERS FOR USE IN CHURCH J. W. G. Masterton The Saint Andrew Press Edinburgh 1970
SBCP	THE SCOTTISH BOOK OF COMMON PRAYER Edinburgh: Cambridge University Press 1929
SJC	LITURGY OF SAINT JOHN CHRYSOSTOM
SM	THE SUNDAY MISSAL Collins 1975
SP	STUDENT PRAYER, Abridged Edition, S.C.M. Press Ltd 1959
SPB	SELECTED PRAYERS Karl Barth, Epworth Press 1966
SS	SERVICES FOR USE IN THE DIOCESE OF SOUTHWARK S.P.C.K. 1926
TC	TOGETHER IN CHURCH Methodist Youth Department 1971
TDS	THE DIVINE SERVICE Committee on Public Worship and Aids to Devotion of the General Assembly of the Church of Scotland, Oxford University Press 1973
UP	THE UNITY BOOK OF PRAYERS Rouillard and Paton Geoffrey Chapman Ltd 1969
VP	VESTRY PRAYERS Prayers original to this collection
WN	WORSHIP NOW Editor David Cairns The Saint Andrew Press Edinburgh 1972